Heroes for Young Readers

Written by Renee Taft Meloche
Illustrated by Bryan Pollard

Adoniram Judson
Amy Carmichael
Betty Greene
Brother Andrew
Cameron Townsend
Corrie ten Boom
C. S. Lewis
David Livingstone
Eric Liddell
George Müller

Gladys Aylward
Hudson Taylor
Jim Elliot
Jonathan Goforth
Loren Cunningham
Lottie Moon
Mary Slessor
Nate Saint
William Carey

Heroes of History for Young Readers

Written by Renee Taft Meloche
Illustrated by Bryan Pollard

Daniel Boone
Clara Barton
George Washington
George Washington Carver
Meriwether Lewis

...and more coming soon

*Heroes for Young Readers Activity Guides and audio CDs
are now available! See the back of this book for more information.*

For a free catalog of books and materials contact
YWAM Publishing, P.O. Box 55787, Seattle, WA 98155
1-800-922-2143 www.ywampublishing.com

HEROES FOR YOUNG READERS

BROTHER ANDREW

Taking Bibles to the World

Written by Renee Taft Meloche
Illustrated by Bryan Pollard

P.O. BOX 55787 SEATTLE, WA 98155

Brother Andrew: Taking Bibles to the World   Text © 2008 by Renee Taft Meloche   Illustrations © 2008 by Bryan Pollard
Published by YWAM Publishing, P.O. Box 55787, Seattle, WA 98155   ISBN 978-1-57658-413-2   Printed in India.   All rights reserved.

A boy named Andrew lived in Holland
    during World War Two.
His country had surrendered to
    the cruel Nazi rule.

Young Andrew looked for ways to help
    his country to be free,
with other Dutch who worked against
    the Nazis secretly.

Though he was only twelve years old,
    he snuck out late at night
and passed out secret messages
    to others in the fight.

He learned that dumping sugar in
    the tanks of Nazi cars
would clog the engines so they could
    not go—at least not far.

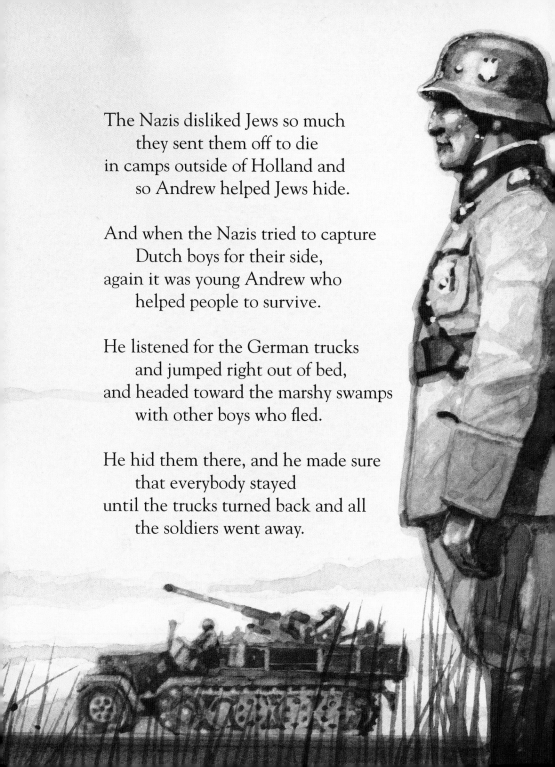

The Nazis disliked Jews so much
    they sent them off to die
in camps outside of Holland and
    so Andrew helped Jews hide.

And when the Nazis tried to capture
    Dutch boys for their side,
again it was young Andrew who
    helped people to survive.

He listened for the German trucks
    and jumped right out of bed,
and headed toward the marshy swamps
    with other boys who fled.

He hid them there, and he made sure
    that everybody stayed
until the trucks turned back and all
    the soldiers went away.

In nineteen forty-five the Nazis
    finally lost the war,
so Andrew looked for new adventures,
    some place to explore.

He joined the army and was shortly
    shipped across the seas
to Dutch-controlled East Indies, where
    he faced new enemies.

His squad was ambushed by the rebels
    who began to shoot.
The bullets whizzed by high and low,
    until one pierced his boot.

The medics put him on a stretcher,
      whisking him away,
straight to a hospital where he
      began a two-month stay.

His ankle had been badly hurt,
      and when he tried to stand,
he had to use a cane, so Andrew
      felt like an old man.

Returning home to Holland, Andrew
    felt so out of place.
He once ran fast but now he limped.
    He'd never win a race.

Although he tried to heal his leg,
    he thought quite gloomily,
There are no more adventures in
    the days ahead of me.

He went to church, not once a week,
    but almost every day,
and started to feel better now
    that he could think and pray.

He had not loved to read the Bible
    when he was a boy,
but now with his new life he found
    the Bible brought him joy.

He went to Christian training school,
and after he was through,
he found a new adventure—one
that he was suited to.

He drove some distance to a country
where the Christians there
could not get jobs or go to school
and Bibles were quite rare.

When Andrew visited a church,
he looked out at the throng
as those with Bibles held them high
so others could look on.

He thought, *It is so easy to
get Bibles in my land.
I must bring them to Christians who
can't get them in their hands.*

In Holland he received a gift—
    a Volkswagen, in blue—
and set out on the mission he
    felt God sent him to do.

He drove to Yugoslavia
    with Bibles that were hidden,
since bringing them inside that country
    strictly was forbidden.

He drove up to the border—
    patrolled by border guards.
They took his passport and they said,
    "Now get out of your car."

The guards searched through his camping gear.
    His heart began to pound.
He'd hidden many Bibles there
    and thought, *What if they're found?*

He'd be arrested if they were.
    He wondered what they'd find.
He prayed, *Lord, you make blind eyes see;*
    now please make seeing eyes blind.

They finished searching through the gear
    and Andrew gave God thanks,
but when they opened up his suitcase,
    Andrew's courage sank.

Beneath his shirts, now in plain view,
    were Bibles packed in there.
As Andrew's hands began to sweat,
    he said another prayer.

Then right away he started up
a friendly conversation.
The guards, distracted, sent him off
to reach his destination.

In Yugoslavia the Bible
stories Andrew knew
were not allowed because the leaders
said they were untrue.

Some people were arrested just
    for hearing Andrew teach.
Despite the danger, growing crowds
    loved hearing God's Word preached.

He gave out all his Bibles, then
    returned home and soon planned
a trip into Bulgaria
    where Bibles, too, were banned.

And after many detours he
    arrived, and for two weeks
he spoke to Christians secretly
    in homes where they would meet.

Each time he gave a Bible out,
    the people's eyes grew bright.
And as the book was passed around,
    their faces filled with light.

Now Andrew wished that he could share
    his mission and his life.
He met a nurse named Corrie and
    she soon became his wife.

He next went to Romania
    to bring them Bibles too,
but wondered at the border line,
    How will I make it through?

He watched as cars ahead were torn
    apart and Andrew knew
his precious Bibles would be found.
    He prayed, *What should I do?*

Soon Andrew felt that he should place
    the Bibles in plain sight—
out in the open, next to him.
    Somehow this just seemed right.

A guard approached and Andrew hoped
    that their eyes would not meet.
The guard looked at his passport, then
    looked down at the front seat.

Although the guard saw stacks of Bibles
    right there on display,
he handed Andrew's passport back
    and waved him on his way!

So Andrew, much relieved, thanked God
    as he continued on.
And soon his Bibles, every one,
    were all completely gone.

He next went into Russia and
    while there a man he met
told him one of the saddest stories
    that he had heard yet.

The man said, "I am from a place
    two thousand miles away,
and there's a special reason why
    I've come to you today.
I had a dream in which I saw
    a gift given to me—
a Bible here in Moscow, an
    impossibility.
The dream I had, though, was so real,
    I came here on my own
because there's not one Bible in
    my church group back at home."

And Andrew was so grateful he
    could make this dream come true
by giving him a Bible—in
    the man's own language, too!

The old man hugged him for the Bible
    and for coming there.
Once just a dream, it now was real—
    an answer to his prayers.

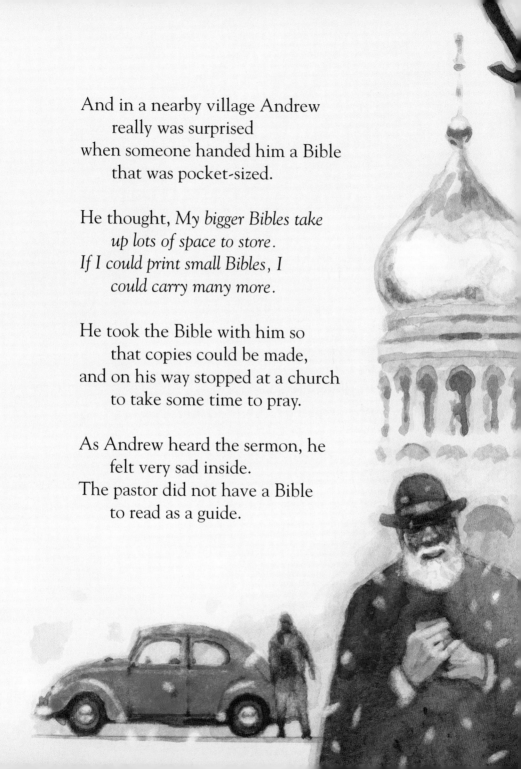

And in a nearby village Andrew
   really was surprised
when someone handed him a Bible
   that was pocket-sized.

He thought, *My bigger Bibles take
   up lots of space to store.
If I could print small Bibles, I
   could carry many more.*

He took the Bible with him so
   that copies could be made,
and on his way stopped at a church
   to take some time to pray.

As Andrew heard the sermon, he
   felt very sad inside.
The pastor did not have a Bible
   to read as a guide.

And Andrew thought, *I wish that there
was something I could do.*
Then he remembered, *I still have
that small one he can use!*

He ran out to his car and found
it under the front seat,
returned and told the pastor, "This
small Bible's yours to keep."

Back home he printed lots of Bibles,
    smaller than before,
and gave his ministry a name.
    He called it "Open Doors."

For years it was not safe for him
    to let too many know
about his secret work but now
    it seemed the time to grow.

Then Andrew went to China, where
    the Christians suffered so.
Soon many other volunteers
    decided they should go.

One million Bibles were brought in
    by boat along the beach.
Then Christians took them secretly
    to places they could meet.

Some lands that once kept Bibles out
    soon changed dramatically,
as people were allowed to practice
    Christianity.

When Russia welcomed Open Doors
    in nineteen eighty-eight,
one million Bibles were passed out—
    good news to celebrate.

And yet the need that Andrew saw
    goes on—there's work to do.
For countries, such as China, still
    have stubbornly refused
to give the people freedom there
    to worship as they choose.
Perhaps we'll be among the ones
    to bring them God's Good News.

Christian Heroes: Then & Now

by Janet and Geoff Benge

Adoniram Judson: Bound for Burma
Amy Carmichael: Rescuer of Precious Gems
Betty Greene: Wings to Serve
Brother Andrew: God's Secret Agent
Cameron Townsend: Good News in Every Language
Clarence Jones: Mr. Radio
Corrie ten Boom: Keeper of the Angels' Den
Count Zinzendorf: Firstfruit
C. S. Lewis: Master Storyteller
C. T. Studd: No Retreat
David Livingstone: Africa's Trailblazer
Eric Liddell: Something Greater Than Gold
Florence Young: Mission Accomplished
George Müller: The Guardian of Bristol's Orphans
Gladys Aylward: The Adventure of a Lifetime
Hudson Taylor: Deep in the Heart of China
Ida Scudder: Healing Bodies, Touching Hearts
Jim Elliot: One Great Purpose
John Wesley: The World His Parish
John Williams: Messenger of Peace
Jonathan Goforth: An Open Door in China
Lillian Trasher: The Greatest Wonder in Egypt
Loren Cunningham: Into All the World
Lottie Moon: Giving Her All for China
Mary Slessor: Forward into Calabar
Nate Saint: On a Wing and a Prayer
Rachel Saint: A Star in the Jungle
Rowland Bingham: Into Africa's Interior
Sundar Singh: Footprints Over the Mountains
Wilfred Grenfell: Fisher of Men
William Booth: Soup, Soap, and Salvation
William Carey: Obliged to Go

Heroes for Young Readers and Heroes of History for Young Readers are based on the Christian Heroes: Then & Now and Heroes of History biographies by Janet and Geoff Benge. Don't miss out on these exciting, true adventures for ages ten and up!

Continued on the next page...

Heroes of History

by Janet and Geoff Benge

Abraham Lincoln: A New Birth of Freedom
Alan Shepard: Higher and Faster
Benjamin Franklin: Live Wire
Christopher Columbus: Across the Ocean Sea
Clara Barton: Courage under Fire
Daniel Boone: Frontiersman
Douglas MacArthur: What Greater Honor
George Washington Carver: From Slave to Scientist
George Washington: True Patriot
Harriet Tubman: Freedombound
John Adams: Independence Forever
John Smith: A Foothold in the New World
Laura Ingalls Wilder: A Storybook Life
Meriwether Lewis: Off the Edge of the Map
Orville Wright: The Flyer
Theodore Roosevelt: An American Original
Thomas Edison: Inspiration and Hard Work
William Penn: Liberty and Justice for All

...and more coming soon. Unit Study Curriculum Guides are also available.

Heroes for Young Readers Activity Guides
Educational and Character-Building Lessons for Children

by Renee Taft Meloche

Heroes for Young Readers Activity Guide for Books 1–4
Gladys Aylward, Eric Liddell, Nate Saint, George Müller

Heroes for Young Readers Activity Guide for Books 5–8
Amy Carmichael, Corrie ten Boom, Mary Slessor, William Carey

Heroes for Young Readers Activity Guide for Books 9–12
Betty Greene, David Livingstone, Adoniram Judson, Hudson Taylor

Heroes for Young Readers Activity Guide for Books 13–16
Jim Elliot, Cameron Townsend, Jonathan Goforth, Lottie Moon

...and more coming soon.

Designed to accompany the vibrant Heroes for Young Readers books, these fun-filled Activity Guides lead young children through a variety of character-building and educational activities. Pick and choose from the activities or follow the included thirteen-week syllabus. An audio CD with book readings, songs, and fun activity tracks is available for each Activity Guide.

For a free catalog of books and materials contact
YWAM Publishing, P.O. Box 55787, Seattle, WA 98155
1-800-922-2143 www.ywampublishing.com